\--

GRANDPA'S SHOE REPAIR SHOP

\--

GRANDPA'S SHOE REPAIR SHOP

BERNICE HUFNAGLE HERNDON

***

Publishing Family

Farmland, Indiana

This book is published by
PUBLISHING FAMILY
Farmland, Indiana

For information about publishing your book, journal,
keepsake or gift, contact

publishing family@ gmail.com

WE PUBLISH FAMILY!

Copyright©2013

ISBN-13 978-0615929880
ISBN 10 0615929885

DEDICATION

For my grandparents, Boydia and Edna (Lewis) Hufnagle for the memories and patience you showed. Just because you were different it did not stop you from being productive people in the world. You worked hard and asked for no handouts and especially not expecting any. Grandma broke a record in 1919 at a factory in Detroit, Michigan that hasn't been broken since, for manual labor. Grandpa did threshing, farming, milkman, umpired for baseball, and shoe repair.

For my parents, Floyd and Barbara (Southcott) Hufnagle and my sisters, Evelyn and Jane for being my family. Love you!

To my children, Christy, Loretta and Jackie, I hope you enjoy my memory of the Shoe Shop and retain some of the family history! Love you! To Jerry, my husband, for his encouragement

To my sisters, hopefully we share some of the same memories. We all see and do things differently. I know you will remember other things that involved you but I hope you will enjoy mine. Love you!

GRANDPA'S SHOE REPAIR SHOP

My Grandpa, Boydia Hufnagle, had a shoe repair shop next to our house in Fremont, Indiana. I lived with my grandparents along with my parents, Floyd and Barbara (Southcott) Hufnagle and 2 sisters, Evelyn and Jane.

Grandpa was born deaf and my Grandma, Edna (Lewis) Hufnagle lost her hearing when she was about 3 years old.

Grandpa also walked with a cane. He injured his leg when he was about 17 years old playing football.

Grandpa retired from farming and sold his half of the farm to his brother Vern. Grandpa and Grandma moved to town and rented a house for a short time. He opened a shoe shop on S. Wayne St. (also known as State Road 827). It was next to the lumber building. They moved to Albion Street, and his shop was just around the corner. Grandpa decided to build a shop next to the house so he and my Dad built the shoe shop in the early 1950's. Grandma worked in the shop with Grandpa.

There were two buildings that were very close to each other and from our house you could see people go between the buildings and drink their whiskey. They didn't want anyone to know they drank I guess. We would go over there to see the different bottles and pour out any that had any whiskey left in them. We were scolded for destroying the contents. We were told to just leave the bottles alone, and to stay out of that area.

BOYDIA AND EDNA HUFNAGLE

BOYD'S SHOE REPAIR SHOP

The shop was made out of cement blocks and had a big picture window and a door with window that was 3/4 of the door and a panel bottom.

When I would walk into the shop I would get a whiff of the leather and a hint of the glue. Sometimes now I can almost smell the leather when I think about it.

Walking in the shop on the left was the leather couch up against the wall for people who needed to sit down. It always looked so worn and I never thought it was very comfortable!

There were always pictures of dogs or cats from past years calendars that hung above the couch. My grandma probably hung the pictures up as she was an animal lover.

GRANDPA'S MISSION COUCH

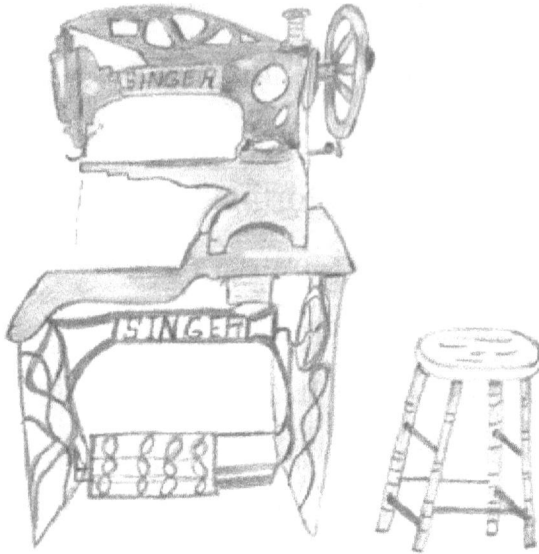

COBBLER'S SEWING MACHINE

The sewing machine was at the end of the couch facing the front door. It was a big sewing machine with thick thread for sewing the leather to the bottom of the shoe.

There was a window beside the sewing machine and you could see the house. Behind the sewing machine was a small round heater.

GRANDPA'S SPITTOON

Grandpa had a spittoon because he chewed tobacco, and his favorite was Union Workman.   My sisters and I would buy Grandpa his Union Workman for Christmas and wrap it up for him to open. He always acted surprised about his gift.   (He always knew what it was).

GRANDPA'S CASH REGISTER

On the right coming in the door was the display case and the cash register sat on top. The cash register was a worn gold color and was tall and the keys sticking out, not flat. Behind the display case was the machinery Grandpa used to repair the shoes.

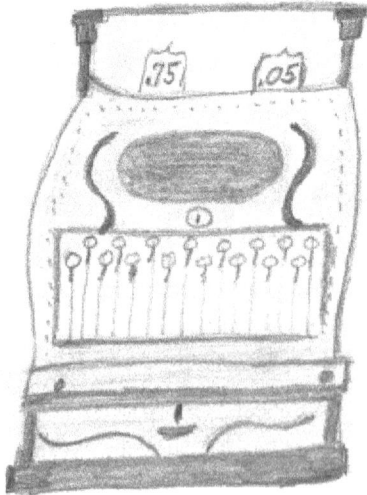

COBBLER'S   MACHINE

At the end of the display case you could get around to the machinery and also to a small walk in closet area where he kept the different sizes of leather soles and heels to repair the shoes. He would sew on the soles and the use a very sharp knife to trim the edge of the leather sole to make a perfect fit to the shoe. Then he would nail on the heel. Before putting on the heel he would put glue on the area first. Then he would smooth the leather after putting on the soles and heels with the machine with the wheels. One of the wheels also would polish the shoes. The finished shoes would look brand new.

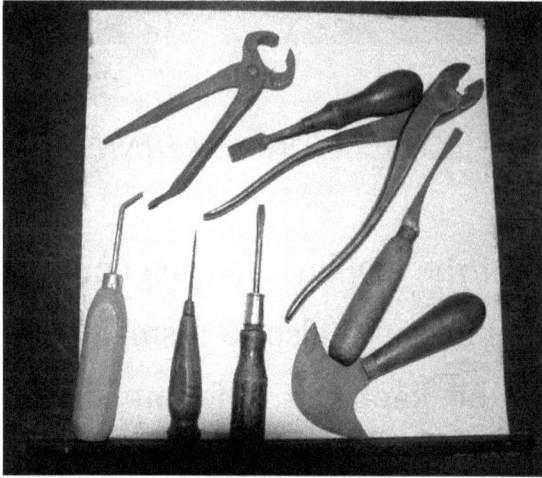

GRANDPA'S   SHOE   REPAIR   TOOLS

GRANDPA AT GENERAL SHOES FINDING CO.
1957

I know of one place that Grandpa went to get supplies for his shop. It was in Toledo, Ohio at the General Shoes Finding Co.

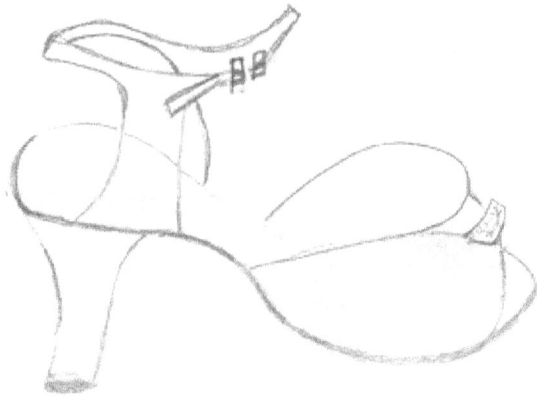

THE   GLASS   SHOE

There was one pair of shoes that I remember.   They
were glass shoes that belonged to a lady in Fremont.
I was fascinated with the shoes as I had never seen
any before.   I thought they should belong to a
princess.   The shoes had been in the shop for a
long time. When Grandpa was closing the shop and
the unclaimed shoes were left, I wanted the glass
shoes so bad. I   asked for them but I was told that
she still might show up to claim them, and she did.

Grandpa was well known by people in and around the area as they always liked the way Grandpa repaired their shoes. Because he couldn't talk, he had paper and pencil to communicate with the customers. He could usually look at the shoes and tell what needed to be done.

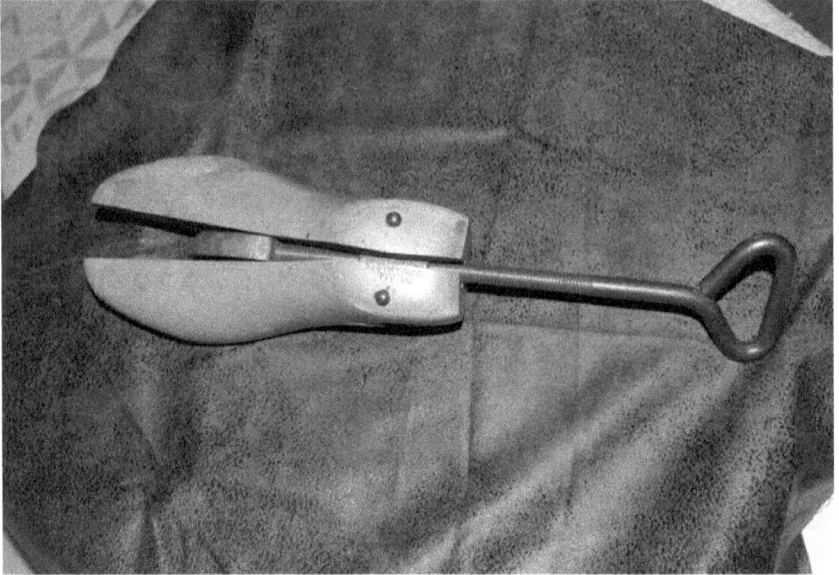

GRANDPA'S SHOE STRETCHER

I remember the scent of the leather and glue. I liked the smell of new leather. I would pick up the lid with the glue brush. If Grandpa caught us doing that he would scold us, and make us leave.

Grandpa would let us play in the area where he kept the leather. There were bins with different sizes of soles and heels. I know we would end up putting them in different bins and getting them all mixed up but I don't remember him ever getting upset over it. We knew never to take any out of the shop and we were never to get into boxes on the top shelf. I couldn't reach them anyway.   We never   knew that was where our parents kept our Christmas presents!

EVELYN, JANE & BERNICE

THE OLD HOUSE

Grandpa said if we ask him for a nickel he would give us one. We could ask for one each day. At that time you could buy a bottle of pop or several pieces of penny candy. You could buy 3 pieces of candy for a penny, or a 3-cent candy bar. I can't remember the name of it but it had a green wrapper. It might have been called "Chocolate Lunch Bar". If you forgot to ask for the nickel that was too bad, you couldn't get 10 cents the next day, you just lost out. Our sign for asking for our nickel, was acting like we were licking an ice cream cone. Well, Grandpa must have been having a bad day when I asked, because he said that I stuck out my tongue at him, so he wouldn't give me my nickel! My heart was almost broken as I would never have stuck out my tongue at him. No amount of explaining to Grandpa would change his mind. Needless to say I did not act like I was licking with my tongue after that.

For Christmas Grandma and Grandpa would give us five dollars wrapped up with a large Hershey candy bar.

Perry Gay purchased the old lumber buildings and tore them down. He built a grocery store, and put in a restaurant and laundromat.   He also purchased the Shoe Repair Shop, so Grandpa retired. That area ended up being the loading dock for Gay's Grocery Store.

My memories of the Shoe Repair Shop will always be a big part of my childhood.

Credits:

Bob & Judy Hummel for letting me take a picture of their cobbler's machine at their Repair Shop in Union City, Indiana.

AUTHOR BIOGRAPHY

Ev, Jane & Bernice on the right with shoes on.
Front steps of the house.   1955

My parents lived in Fremont, Indiana where my dad was from, and they lived with dad's parents. Mom was from Coldwater, Michigan and that was where her doctor was, so when it was time for me to me born she went back to Coldwater, Michigan. I am a Wolverine by birth, and   was raised a Hoosier in a county with 101 lakes.

I credit my grandmother for my interest in family history. When I was 8 years old she would show me items that belonged to the family, and tell me the history and who it belonged to. When I was 14 grandma's sister, Aunt Ina, introduced me to a family tree, and she let me help her in putting down some information. I was hooked! Family genealogy is my addiction!

I met my husband in Angola, Indiana, while I was working at a drive-in restaurant named Sandy's. After we were married we lived at Pleasant Lake, Indiana, for about 6 years, and then moved to Farmland, Indiana. We have 3 beautiful daughters, 7 adorable grandchildren and 2 charming great-grandchildren.

I worked for the Town of Farmland as Deputy Clerk-Treasurer for 12 ½ years, and then ran the office as Clerk-Treasurer for 17 years before I retired. I am enjoying my grandchildren. I like to read and travel.

I am a breast cancer survivor!

The pencil drawings are the very first time I have done it. Maybe I should take an art lesson so I know what I am doing! This book is a surprise for my sisters, so I could not ask the artist of the family to do my drawings.

December,   2013

www.ingramcontent.com/pod-product-compliance
Lightning Source LLC
Chambersburg PA
CBHW060601030426
42337CB00019B/3581